INDIVIDUALIZED EDUCATIONAL PROGRAMMING (IEP)

IEP   22

author

judy a. schrag, ed.d.

series editor
thomas n. fairchild, ph.d.

illustrator
bart l. miller

Teaching Resources
A New York Times Company

individualized educational programming (iep):
a child study team process

by
judy a. schrag
idaho state department of education

thomas n. fairchild
series editor

bart l. miller
illustrator

Andrew S. Thomas Memorial Library
MORRIS HARVEY COLLEGE, CHARLESTON, W.VA.
Teaching Resources Corporation
100 Boylston Street, Boston, Massachusetts 02116, 617-357-8446

Library of Congress Cataloging in Publication Data

Schrag, Judy A
   Individualized educational programming (IEP)

   (Mainstreaming series)
   1. Exceptional children—Education.   2   Individualized
instruction.   I. Title.
LC3969.S35   371.9'043   77-4431
ISBN 0-89384-019-X

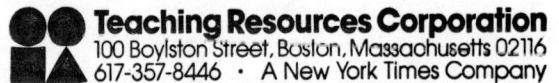

Teaching Resources Corporation
100 Boylston Street, Boston, Massachusetts 02116
617-357-8446 · A New York Times Company

This book is dedicated to all children with special needs...with the hope that they will benefit from carefully planned educational programming.

acknowledgments

Individualized Educational Programming (IEP) is currently a consideration of many people across the nation who are attempting to implement federal legislation, Public Law 94-142, as well as specific state legislation in behalf of exceptional children. I would like to express my appreciation to those who have developed papers related to IEP, in particular the National Association of State Directors of Special Education (NASDSE). These papers stand as a base of knowledge upon which this manuscript is partially based.

Also a special thanks. . .

To Dr. Tom Fairchild for his careful editing.

To Dr. Fairchild and his wife, Carolyn; and to Anne Gross for their many creative cartoon ideas.

To Bart Miller, illustrator, for bringing the cartoon ideas to life.

To Shellie West for excellent typing assistance.

I would also like to thank my husband, Howard, and son, Mike, for their encouragement and support.

Judy A. Schrag

preface

In the past, educational needs of exceptional children were met by removing them from the "mainstream" of regular classes and serving them in a variety of segregated, self-contained special classes. The trend in the '70's is educating exceptional children in the least restrictive educational setting; that is, as closely as possible to their normal peers. This concept of mainstreaming exceptional children has received considerable support from within and outside the educational community. Although self-contained special classes will always be a meaningful alternative for some children, the personal and educational needs of many exceptional children can be better served in the regular class program with the supportive services of ancillary personnel and/or resource room help.

With the emphasis on mainstreaming, the regular class teacher is now expected to meet the needs of exceptional children in his or her classroom along with all the other children in the class. The problem is that most regular class teachers have little or no preparation in the area of educating exceptional children. Regular class teachers need basic information regarding the various exceptionalities, and more specifically, practical suggestions which they can employ to enhance the mainstreamed exceptional child's personal and educational development. Teachers also need to learn to develop an Individualized Educational Program (IEP) since this is one of the most important tasks to be completed by a Child Study Team.

The MAINSTREAMING SERIES was written to fill these needs. Most of the books in the SERIES address themselves to specific areas of exceptionality, allowing teachers to select from the SERIES according to their interests or needs. These texts provide information designed to eliminate misconceptions and stereotypes and to improve the teacher's understanding of the exceptional child's uniqueness. Numerous practical suggestions are offered which will help the teacher work more effectively with the exceptional child in the mainstream of the regular class. Other texts in the SERIES focus on working with parents, the public law, and developing an individualized educational program for an exceptional child.

Currently, there is a great deal of controversy surrounding the use of categories and labels. The books in the SERIES are organized according to categories of exceptionality because the content within each book is only relevant for a specific handicapping condition. The intent is not to propagate labeling; in fact, labeling children is inconsistent with the philosophy of the SERIES. The books address themselves to behaviors and how teachers can work with these behaviors in exceptional children. The books in the SERIES are categorized—not the children. The books are categorized in order to cue teachers to the particular content for which they might be looking.

There is much truth to the old saying, "A picture is worth a thousand words." A cartoon format was used for each book in the MAINSTREAMING SERIES as a means of sustaining interest and emphasizing important concepts. The cartoon format also allows for easy, relaxed reading. We felt that teachers, being on the firing line all day, would be more likely to read and refer to our material than to a lengthy text filled with theory and jargon. Typical to cartooning is the need to exaggerate, stereotype, and focus on our weaknesses. I sincerely hope the cartoons do not offend any children, parents, or professionals, because that is not the purpose for which they were intended. They are intended to help you think.

I hope you find this book helpful in your work with mainstreamed exceptional children, or with any other children, since they are all special.

THOMAS N. FAIRCHILD
SERIES EDITOR

introduction

The purpose of this book is to facilitate an understanding of the concept of Individualized Educational Programming (IEP) and to describe a process for its implementation. The rationale for the development of an IEP as well as the role and functions of a Child Study Team are presented. The components of an IEP and the process that a Child Study Team may follow to develop and implement IEP's are detailed.

It is my hope that this book will assist you in the implementation of quality educational programs for exceptional children.

contents

chapter 1

---

why is there a need for an individualized educational program?

The Individualized Educational Program (IEP) is a requirement of the federal Education for All Handicapped Children Act (Public Law 94-142). This law requires that all children, regardless of the type and extent of handicaps, be provided a free appropriate public education and/or related services as needed to meet their unique learning needs.

An integral provision within this law requires that an IEP be written for each exceptional child who is receiving or will receive special education, regardless of the institution or agency providing the services.

The concept of Individualized Educational Programming (IEP) has parallels in other federal legislation. P.L. 94-103, the 1976 Amendments to the Developmental Disabilities Act, requires that services be provided according to an Individualized Program Plan (IPP). The 1974 Amendments to the Vocational Rehabilitation Act, P.L. 93-112, similarly assure the provision of an Individualized Rehabilitation Plan (IRP).

The development and use of Individualized Programs (IEP's, IPP's, or IRP's) assure that children with special learning needs will have greater opportunities for successful educational experiences. The use of IEP's helps educators and other service providers tailor their teaching and training procedures to the individual student's strengths and weaknesses.

Many educators working with exceptional children have been developing and implementing IEP's for years. However, the concept of an IEP as described in P.L. 94-142 is somewhat broader than traditional individualization of instruction.

The definition of an appropriate education has been extended to include the provision of related services which may involve speech pathology, audiology, psychological services, physical therapy, occupational therapy, transportation, recreation, . . .

. . .therapeutic recreation, counseling services, medical services, early identification and assessment, and other services as needed by each child.

Another modification of past practices is the attempt to move away from categorical placement and programming. Placement decisions will be based on educational planning for each child as well as parental involvement.

THE IEP INDICATES THAT HERBIE SHOULD REMAIN IN YOUR REGULAR CLASSROOM FOR THE FULL DAY.

AAAAAAAAAA

This should help eradicate the traditional practice of determining that a child is eligible for special education and/or related services because he/she falls within a medical classification or label such as trainable mentally retarded or learning disabilities. Subsequently, the child would then have been placed in a classroom for that "type of child," only to be followed with the development of an "individualized" program within that placement. Thus, the use of IEP's written *prior to* placement suggests a new order in decision-making.

The use of IEP's along with other evaluation procedures provide administrators with excellent vehicles to monitor the effectiveness of services provided based on the educational progress made by each student.

Information compiled concerning the needs of exceptional students also assists administrators in making appropriate decisions regarding allocation of resources.

Annual and continued monitoring also allows for needed modifications to insure that individual learning objectives are being appropriately addressed. IEP's are a way to operationalize "appropriate" education as required by P.L. 94-142.

chapter 2

---

what is an individualized educational program?

An Individualized Educational Program (IEP) is a statement written for each exceptional child. At a minimum, it should contain certain components as specified by the regulations for P.L. 94-142.

PRESENT LEVEL OF EDUCATIONAL PERFORMANCE:

ROTTEN

One such component is a description of the child's present level of educational performance.

Another component is the specification of annual goals. . .

IEP

SHORT TERM OBJECTIVES:

For the week beginning 5/2/77, Herbie will be locked out of class each morning.

. . .and short-term objectives.

SPECIFIC EDUCATIONAL SERVICES TO BE PROVIDED:

1. Remedial snow-shoveling.
2. Grp. window washing.
3. Self-contained cafeteria clean-up.

The specific educational services to be provided must be outlined as well as. . .

. . .the extent to which the child will participate in the regular classroom.

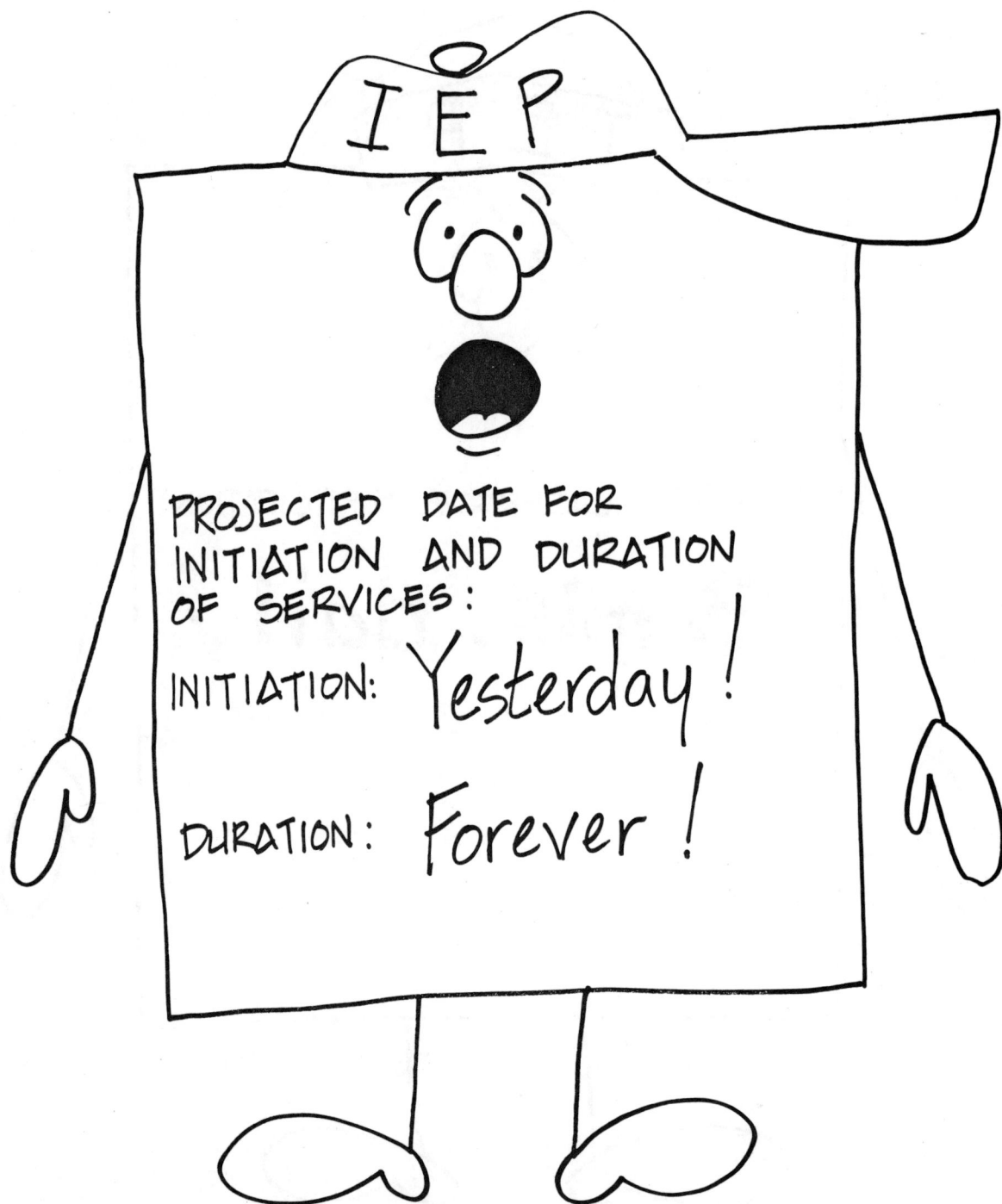

PROJECTED DATE FOR INITIATION AND DURATION OF SERVICES:

INITIATION: Yesterday!

DURATION: Forever!

Another component of the IEP required by P.L. 94-142 is the projected date for initiation and duration of services.

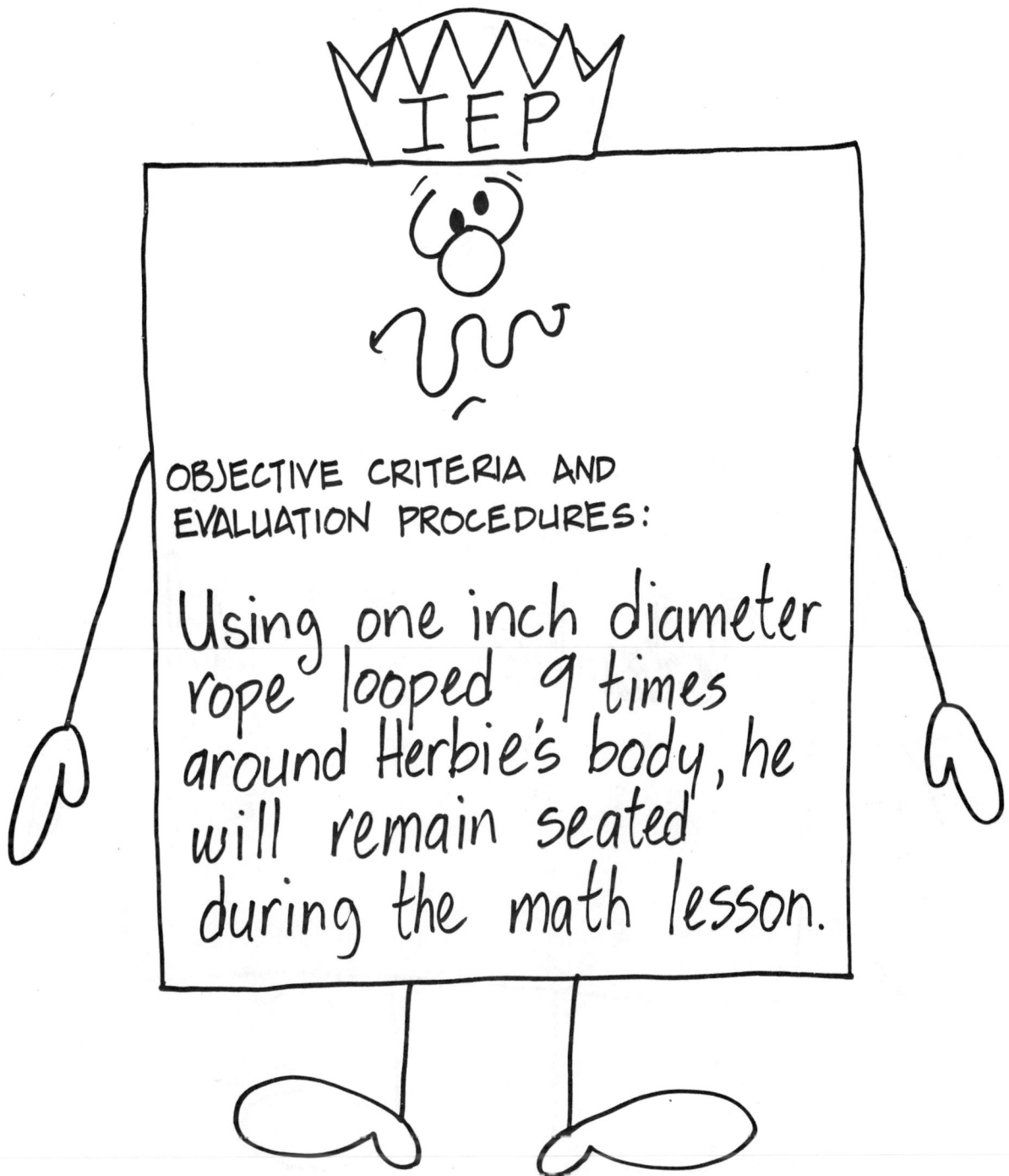

OBJECTIVE CRITERIA AND
EVALUATION PROCEDURES:

Using one inch diameter
rope looped 9 times
around Herbie's body, he
will remain seated
during the math lesson.

Objective criteria and evaluation procedures must also
be included.

SCHEDULE AND PROCEDURES
FOR REVIEW:

Octember 33rd!

The final component specified by P.L. 94-142 is a description of the schedule and procedures for review of the IEP. This review must occur at least annually.

An IEP can be thought of as having three levels:

1. Total Service Plan
2. Implementation/Instructional Plan
3. Annual Review

Level one: The IEP: Total Service Plan is designed to guide educational planning from the level of the Child Study Team. It is a general statement of goals, or a framework for more specific, short-term objectives and program plans. A Total Service Plan contains:

- Annual goals
- Summary statement(s) of present level of student performance
- Extent to which the child will participate in the regular class
- Recommendation for educational placement (This should include the legal category of exceptionality for which the child qualifies for state and/or federal funding, if appropriate. Such a label should only be used for funding and *not* for programming purposes.)
- Overall educational or related services to be provided
- Projected date for initiation and duration of planned services
- General recommendations concerning appropriate methods and materials
- Overall evaluation criteria to be utilized

The Child Study Team is primarily responsible for the development of the IEP: Total Service Plan.

INDIVIDUALIZED EDUCATIONAL PROGRAM: TOTAL SERVICE PLAN

Local Education Agency:
Name and Number _____

School _____

Name of Student _____

Date of Birth _____ Age _____ Grade _____

Summary of Present Levels of Student Performance: _____

Description of Educational Placement Recommendation:

	Hrs/Week		Hrs/Week	Legal Category of Exceptionality (for funding purposes only)
Special Education Program Model _____		Regular Education _____		_____

Program Goal(s)	Specific Special Education and/or Related Services	Person(s) Responsible For Implementation	Hours Per Week	Starting Date	Projected Ending Date	Annual Review Date (Mo-Yr)	Child Study Team Recommendations: Methods & Materials— (If appropriate)	Evaluation Criteria

CHILD STUDY TEAM MEMBERS PRESENT

Signature	Position
_____	_____
_____	_____
_____	_____
_____	_____

Agreement with IEP: Total Service Plan
(Check appropriate space)

YES _____   NO _____

Date of
Child Study
Team Meeting: _____

INDIVIDUALIZED EDUCATIONAL PROGRAM: TOTAL SERVICE PLAN

Local Education Agency:
Name and Number _____ *Marshton* _____ *111* _____

School _____ *Jefferson Elementary* _____

Name of Student _____ *Jimmy Smith* _____

Date of Birth _____ *9-1-70* _____ Age _____ *6-0* _____ Grade _____ *1* _____

Description of Educational Placement Recommendation:

	Hrs/Week
Special Education Program Model *Self-Contained Classroom*	*30*
Regular Education *NA*	
	0

Legal Category of
Exceptionality (for
funding purposes only)

Trainable Mentally

Retarded

Summary of Present Levels of Student Performance:

Although Jimmy has a chronological age of 6-0, his mental age is 3-5 and language age is 3-2. He demonstrates very few self-help and communication skills. His IQ as measured on an individual test of intelligence is approximately 45.

Program Goal(s)	Specific Special Education and/or Related Services	Person(s) Responsible For Implementation	Hours Per Week	Starting Date	Projected Ending Date	Annual Review Date (Mo-Yr)	Child Study Team Recommendations: Methods & Materials— (If appropriate)	Evaluation Criteria
Student will demonstrate the ability to eat, to drink, and to perform basic dressing skills independently	Physical Therapy Special Education Classroom	Ms. Brown Ms. Smith	2½ 30	10-1-76 9-15-76	5-15-77 5-15-77	5-15-77 5-15-77		Student will eat, drink, and dress independently.
Student will develop simple expressive language skills.	Speech Therapy	Mr. Thomas	5	10-1-76	5-15-77	5-15-77	Peabody Language Development Kit	Given a verbal or picture cue, student will demonstrate a vocabulary of 50 words

CHILD STUDY TEAM MEMBERS PRESENT

Signature	Position	Agreement with IEP: Total Service Plan (Check appropriate space)	
		YES	NO
Mr. John Aahe	Principal	X	
Mr. Sally Smith	Teacher	X	
Mrs. Jack Smith	Parent	X	
Mr. Harold Thomas	Speech Therapist	X	
Mrs. Nola Brown	Physical Therapist	X	

Date of
Child Study
Team Meeting:
9-10-76

After the Total Service Plan has been completed, the IEP enters the **second level** of development. For each of the service or program areas listed on the Total Service Plan, teachers and/or other school personnel will be responsible for developing and carrying through an IEP: Implementation/Instructional Plan. This Implementation Plan will contain:

- More specific program objectives
- Strategies and instructional techniques
- Specific materials and resources
- Criteria for achievement of implementation/ instructional objectives
- Date objectives are initiated and completed

The Child Study Team is ultimately responsible for the development of this level of the IEP. It will continually monitor the child's progress to assure that the Total Service Plan is being carried out through the specific Implementation/Instructional Plans.

INDIVIDUALIZED EDUCATIONAL PROGRAM: IMPLEMENTATION/INSTRUCTIONAL PLAN

Name of Student _____ Date of Birth _____ Age _____ Grade _____ School _____

Local Education
Agency
Name & No. _____

Date of Entry Into Program _____ Projected Ending Date _____

(Signature of Implementor Completing this Form)

Program Goal(s)	Implementation/Instructional Objectives	Strategies and/or Techniques	Materials and/or Resources	Date Started	Date Ended	Criteria for Mastery of each Implementation/ Instructional Objective

28

INDIVIDUALIZED EDUCATIONAL PROGRAM: IMPLEMENTATION/INSTRUCTIONAL PLAN

Name of Student Jimmy Smith

Date of Birth 9-1-70   Age 6-0   Grade 1   School Jefferson

Local Education Agency Name & No. Marshton   111

Date of Entry Into Program 9-15-76   Projected Ending Date 5-15-77

(Signature of Implementor Completing this Form)

Program Goal(s)	Implementation/Instructional Objectives	Strategies and/or Techniques	Materials and/or Resources	Date Started	Date Ended	Criteria for Mastery of each Implementation/Instructional Objective
Student will demonstrate the ability to eat, to drink, and to perform basic dressing skills independently.	Student will unbutton a garment independently.	Techniques used will emphasize short verbal commands & modeling of appropriate behavior.	Teacher Made Materials	9-15-76	In Progress	Objectives will be performed at 95% accuracy.
	Student will independently put on cap/hat.			9-15-76	10-1-76	
	Student will zip a closed-ended zipper independently.			9-15-76	10-1-76	
	Student will unbuckle independently.			9-15-76	11-15-76	
	Student will drink from a cup independently.			9-15-76	1-15-77	
	Student will eat soft and hard foods independently.			9-15-76	2-15-77	

29

INDIVIDUALIZED EDUCATIONAL PROGRAM: IMPLEMENTATION/INSTRUCTIONAL PLAN

Name of Student ___Jimmy Smith___   Date of Birth ___2-1-70___   Age ___6-0___   Grade ___1___   School ___Jefferson___

Date of Entry Into Program ___10-1-76___   Projected Ending Date ___2-1-77___

Local Education Agency Name & No. ___Marshton   111___

(Signature of Implementor Completing this Form)

Program Goal(s)	Implementation/Instructional Objectives	Strategies and/or Techniques	Materials and/or Resources	Date Started	Date Ended	Criteria for Mastery of each Implementation/ Instructional Objective
Student will develop simple expressive language skills.	Student will identify words of 25 familiar objects when paired with their pictures.	Presentation of familiar object with printed word below picture, with explanation of relationship between word and picture. Student will point to picture and verbally label picture and printed word.	Peabody Language Development Kit - Level P Teacher Made Materials	10-15-76	In Progress	Student will identify words of 25 familiar objects when paired with their pictures with 90% accuracy.
	Student will identify 25 printed words and match to the appropriate objects.	Presentation of object in front of student along with printed word. Student will verbally label printed word and match it to the object.	See Above	1-15-77	In Progress	Student will identify 25 printed words and match to the appropriate objects with 90% accuracy.

30

Short-term objectives and ongoing measurement included within the Implementation/Instructional Plan serve as a basis for **level three** of the IEP: Annual Review. The purpose of the IEP: Annual Review is to determine the appropriateness of the child's educational program (levels one and two of the IEP) as determined by his/her progress toward short-term objectives and annual goals. The Child Study Team has the major responsibility for carrying out an Annual Review of each child's progress.

An option at this level of IEP development is either to review the original Total Service Plan and Implementation/Instructional plan and to revise as necessary on the Annual Review form, *or* to complete a new Total Service Plan. The review can best be conducted in late spring to accommodate planning for the fall program.

INDIVIDUALIZED EDUCATIONAL PROGRAM: ANNUAL REVIEW

Name of Student _____ Date of Birth _____ Age _____ Grade _____ School _____

Local Education Agency
Name and Number _____ Date of Annual Review _____

IEP: Total Service Plan and
Implementation/Instructional Components:

	Level of Appropriateness (Check appropriate space)		Recommended Change:
	YES	NO	
Special Education Placement	_____	_____	_____
Regular Education Placement	_____	_____	_____
Specific Special Education and/or Related Services	_____	_____	_____
Program Goal(s)	_____	_____	_____
Implementation/Instructional Short-term Objective(s)	_____	_____	_____
Specific Materials and/or Resources	_____	_____	_____
Specific Teaching Strategies and/or Techniques	_____	_____	_____
Evaluation Criteria for Completion of Program Goal(s)	_____	_____	_____
Evaluation Criteria for Completion of Implementation/Instructional Objective(s)	_____	_____	_____

CHILD STUDY TEAM MEMBERS PRESENT

		Agreement of Annual Review (Check appropriate space)	
		YES	NO
Signature	Position		
_____	_____	_____	_____
_____	_____	_____	_____
_____	_____	_____	_____
_____	_____	_____	_____

32

INDIVIDUALIZED EDUCATIONAL PROGRAM: ANNUAL REVIEW

Name of Student _Jimmy Smith_ Date of Birth _9-1-70_ Age _6-0_ Grade _1_ School _Jefferson Elementary_

Local Education Agency _Marshton_
Name and Number _111_ Date of Annual Review _5-15-77_

IEP: Total Service Plan and
Implementation/Instructional Components:

Recommended Change:

Level of Appropriateness
(Check appropriate space)

	YES	NO
Special Education Placement	X	
Regular Education Placement		X
Specific Special Education and/or Related Services	X		Add physical education and recreation - 1½ hours weekly
Program Goal(s)	X	
Implementation/Instructional Short-term Objective(s)		X	Add: Student will be able to name each of the 21 consonants and each of the five vowels upon presentation of their sounds.
Specific Materials and/or Resources	X	
Specific Teaching Strategies and/or Techniques	X	.
Evaluation Criteria for Completion of Program Goal(s)		
Evaluation Criteria for Completion of Implementation/Instructional Objective(s)		

CHILD STUDY TEAM MEMBERS PRESENT

Signature	Position	Agreement of Annual Review (Check appropriate space)	
		YES	NO
mr. John Ochre	Principal	X	
ms. Sally Smith	Teacher	X	
mrs. Jack Smith	Parent	X	
mr. Harold Thomas	Speech Therapist	X	
mrs. Viola Brown	Physical Therapist	X	

33

INDIVIDUALIZED EDUCATIONAL PROGRAMS

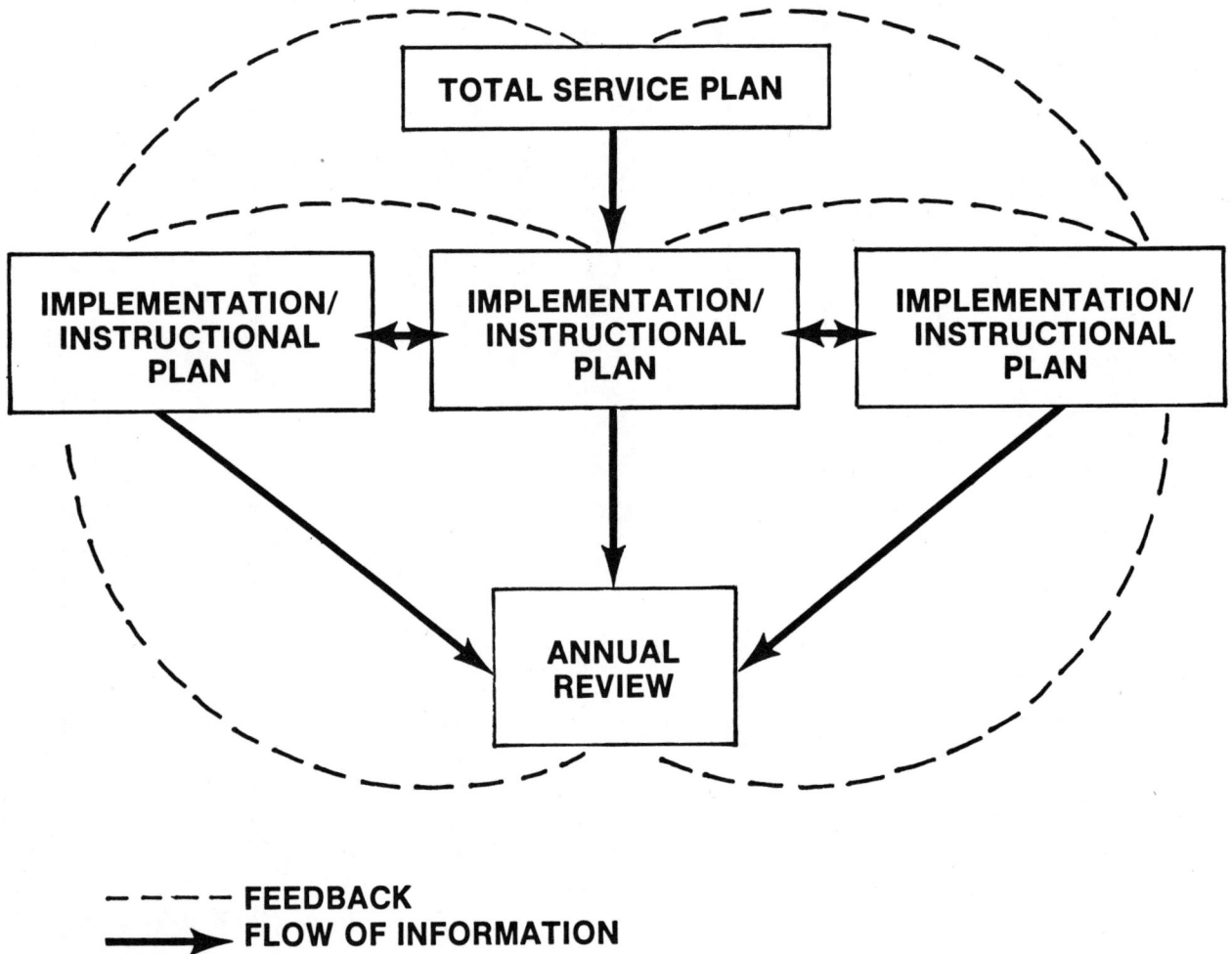

```
                    ┌─────────────────────────┐
                    │   TOTAL SERVICE PLAN     │
                    └─────────────────────────┘
                                │
                                ▼
┌──────────────────┐  ┌──────────────────┐  ┌──────────────────┐
│ IMPLEMENTATION/  │◄►│ IMPLEMENTATION/  │◄►│ IMPLEMENTATION/  │
│ INSTRUCTIONAL    │  │ INSTRUCTIONAL    │  │ INSTRUCTIONAL    │
│     PLAN         │  │     PLAN         │  │     PLAN         │
└──────────────────┘  └──────────────────┘  └──────────────────┘
          │                    │                    │
           ╲                   ▼                   ╱
            ╲        ┌──────────────────┐        ╱
             ╲──────►│      ANNUAL      │◄──────╱
                     │      REVIEW      │
                     └──────────────────┘
```

– – – – FEEDBACK
───────► FLOW OF INFORMATION

It should be noted that the three levels of IEP's are interdependent and closely related. The Total Service Plan flows into more specific Implementation/Instructional Plans and both of these are evaluated by the Annual Review (third level).

chapter 3

**who makes up the
child study team and
how is it organized?**

The purpose of utilizing a Child Study Team as opposed to an individual in decision-making is to provide a broad range of competencies and shared responsibility for educational planning.

The Child Study Team will involve individuals who have the authority to support educational decisions, individuals who will implement decisions, and individuals who will benefit from services provided.

Child Study Teams, or groups of individuals who are responsible for educational programs for exceptional children, presently function under such diverse titles as: Placement Committees, Admissions and Discharge Committees, Student Support Teams, Personnel Guidance Teams, Core Evaluation Teams, Public Evaluation Teams, Case Conference Teams, Staffing Teams, and so on.

The membership of a Child Study Team will vary from state to state, local education agency to local education agency, and child to child. The child's needs will define the membership of a Child Study Team; . . .

. . .however, at a minimum the Team will include the person who referred the child, . . .

. . .the person who will implement a program for the child (e.g., the teacher), . . .

. . .the person who evaluates the child (e.g., the psychologist, communication disorders specialist, etc.), . . .

. . .and the person who is responsible for the administration of the program (e.g., the superintendent, principal, or director of special education.)

42

Parents must also be invited to participate as members of the Child Study Team. Parental input will expand the team's understanding of the child's needs. Involvement of the child's parents will also result in better understanding and increased cooperation.

Remember, if the parents do not participate in the formal Child Study Team placement meeting, their written consent and agreement is required for any major change in the educational placement of their child. Parents must also provide written consent before a comprehensive evaluation is conducted on their child prior to the development of the IEP.

Whenever feasible and appropriate, the child should also be included as a member of the Child Study Team. Composition of the team can vary depending on what evaluations are to be conducted, which decisions will be made, what the policies of the state or local education agency are, etc.

The Child Study Team's function begins when a child has been formally referred for special education and/or related services and continues as long as the child progresses through the program. The numerous functions of the team will typically involve responsibilities in the following areas:

Training
Organization
Leadership
Recording
Due Process
Screening
Comprehensive Evaluation
IEP Development
Evaluation

TRAINING

Once Child Study Teams have been initially organized on a school district or building level, the members should receive in-service training on how to function effectively as an interdisciplinary team. Training should emphasize roles and activities of a Child Study Team, goals of regular education, special education and/or related services, eligibility criteria for such services, educational delivery alternatives, requirements of due process, and other decision-making and evaluative functions.

The local education agency superintendent or appropriate administrator is responsible for providing in-service training to the Child Study Team as well as to the entire school district staff. This promotes visibility of the Child Study Team process and makes teachers and other school personnel aware of the benefits this process can provide.

ORGANIZATION

The Child Study Team should make sure all organizational duties are carried out: scheduling and making other arrangements for team meetings; . . .

. . .providing information on state and district eligibility criteria, assessment guidelines, and placement options; . . .

. . .and making available any resource material needed by team members.

LEADERSHIP

Chairing team meetings is an important responsibility. Because the principal is the instructional leader of the building, it is important for him or her to chair the Child Study Team meetings whenever possible. He or she may delegate responsibility for choosing the leader of the team. However, the principal will maintain ultimate responsibility for the team's functioning.

RECORDING

As much as we all hate paperwork, it is essential for the smooth functioning of a Child Study Team. Recording responsibilities include preparation and organization of all forms: . . .

Referral Form
Parent permission for comprehensive evaluations
Parent permission for placement (may be replaced by IEP: Total Service Plan)
Parent permission for change of educational program
IEP: Total Service Plan
IEP: Implementation/Instructional Plan
IEP: Annual Review
Access log for the management of student records
Release forms for student records for use by other agencies

. . .keeping records of team meetings, and supervising or maintaining appropriate central and classroom files.

DUE PROCESS

The Child Study Team is responsible for insuring that due process procedures have been adhered to regarding individual assessment, IEP development, educational placement, maintenance of student records, and availability of informal or formal hearing procedures.

SCREENING

The screening function of the Child Study Team includes early identification of learning problems, . . .

. . .prioritizing referrals, and reviewing available data to make recommendations for comprehensive evaluations when necessary.

COMPREHENSIVE EVALUATION

The Child Study Team assures that a comprehensive evaluation is conducted and prepares a written report which provides sufficient information for making appropriate educational decisions.

The comprehensive evaluation procedures that are required vary from state to state. Check your state's guidelines as well as your local education agency's policies.

IEP DEVELOPMENT

The team is responsible for preparing the IEP: Total Service Plan which specifies the programs and/or services essential for meeting the child's individual needs. Individual Child Study Team members develop IEP: Implementation Plans according to their designated responsibilities in working with the child.

EVALUATION

The team is responsible for assuring that progress data is kept for the child and for determining the appropriateness of the Total Service Plan and/or Implementation Plans. Ongoing evaluations (continuous assessment) will be an integral part of the Implementation Plan; however, a formal annual review is mandatory.

This review assures that program goals and objectives are being met, that implementors are held accountable for carrying out their program responsibilities, and that any program changes will be based on the results of ongoing accumulation of data.

Another evaluation responsibility that the team should not overlook is the one of their effectiveness as a team! Changes in team assignments, organizational procedures, functions and activities, and even composition may be made as a result of a team's self-evaluation.

In order to assure effective team functioning and efficiency, goals and team responsibilities should be established. These decisions should be in writing and agreed upon by all members. One format that may be utilized to delegate team responsibilities is:

CHILD STUDY TEAM RESPONSIBILITIES

Student: _____

TEAM MEMBER	NAME	Training	Organization	Leadership	Recording	Due Process	Screening	Comprehensive Evaluations	IEP Development	Evaluation	COMMENTS (Date of responsibility, logistics, etc.)
Person Referring											
Principal or Designee											
Special Education Director or Designee											
Special Education Teacher											
Regular Class Teacher											
Parents											
School Psychologist											
Consulting Teacher											
Communication Disorders Specialist											
Counselor											
School Nurse											
Other											

chapter 4

---

how can an individualized educational program be developed and implemented by the child study team?

During the past several years, there has been a growing concern for educators and other service providers to be held accountable for providing quality educational services for exceptional children. Recent court decisions as well as the passage of state and federal laws have reflected this concern.

Federal legislation, P.L. 94-142, outlines procedures for carrying out sound educational planning at the local level:

1. The formation of a group of individuals or a team with specific decision-making responsibilities concerning each exceptional child.

2. The development, by this team, of an IEP which is based on an assessment or evaluation of the child's educational needs.

A group of individuals such as a Child Study Team can develop the IEP, facilitate its implementation, and evaluate its success. In addition, they can *support* individuals who will carry out other instructional programs or related services for the child.

The functions and activities carried out by a Child Study Team provide due process safeguards for the child, the parents, and the school. The IEP assures that educational planning is responsive to the needs of the child. It also establishes standards or criteria for evaluating the appropriateness of the educational programs and services provided for the child.

In the development and implementation of IEP's, Child Study Teams carry out a process or sequence of activities.

Team Reviews Appropriate Information Concerning The Child's Educational Functioning

After the Child Study Team receives a referral for special education services,. . .

. . .the team must gather and review the necessary information in order to make appropriate educational decisions.

It is the team's responsibility to review existing information for its adequacy in determining the child's eligibility for special education and/or related services, to determine appropriate educational placement for the child and to develop an IEP: Total Service Plan.

Information to be collected, summarized, and analyzed will be obtained from a variety of sources to assure that a comprehensive evaluation of the child's characteristics, levels of performance, and educational needs are considered.

Several sources of existing information may be utilized, such as. . .

. . .school and social agency records and. . .

. . .medical records.

Data from achievement tests, . . .

. . .and developmental scales enhance the team's understanding of the child's needs.

74

Other records of diagnostic evaluations conducted by specialists. . .

. . .plus information obtained from diagnostic interviews provide further important data when conducting a comprehensive evaluation.

And don't forget - direct observation. It is one of the best assessment tools we have.

Team Conducts Or Arranges For Additional Testing As Necessary

The team determines if any additional information or evaluation is needed in order to develop an adequate profile of the child's needs.

Caution: Evaluation instruments and procedures should be selected with care. The child should not be labeled on the basis of a single test result.

If additional testing is necessary, the Child Study Team must secure written permission *prior* to conducting the individual evaluation.

POSSIBLE AREAS FOR CHILD EVALUATION*

1. Educational Assessment
   a. Pupil progress in specific skill areas
   b. Achievement in subject areas
   c. Learning style
   d. Strengths and weaknesses

2. Social-Emotional Assessment
   a. Social-psychological development
      1) Attending-receiving
      2) Responding
      3) Valuing
      4) Organizing
      5) Characterizing
   b. Self-help skills

3. Physical Assessment
   a. Visual
   b. Hearing
   c. Speech
   d. Motor-psychomotor
      1) Gross motor
      2) Fine motor
   e. Medical health

4. Cognitive Assessment
   a. Intelligence
   b. Adaptive behavior
   c. Thinking processes
      1) Knowledge
      2) Comprehension
      3) Application
      4) Analysis
      5) Synthesis
      6) Evaluation

5. Language Assessment
   a. Receptive
   b. Expressive
   c. Nonverbal
   d. Speech

6. Family
   a. Dominant language
   b. Parent-child interactions
   c. Social service needs

7. Environment
   a. Home
   b. School
   c. Interpersonal
   d. Material

*Note: Reprinted with permission from Russell, et al. (1976).

Throughout the process of obtaining and reviewing information, the Child Study Team must assure *procedural safeguards* which include due process, . . .

. . .nondiscriminatory screening/testing relative to race, culture, and socio-economic status, . . .

. . .and confidential access to student records. Only authorized school personnel, including parents or guardians, should have the opportunity to review and inspect student records.

①

②

Team Determines Eligibility

After the Child Study Team has reviewed all appropriate information, as well as the results of any additional evaluations, it must determine whether the child is eligible and in need of special education and/or related services. Local, state, and/or federal eligibility criteria might be reviewed and utilized in determining eligibility and the extent of needed services.

84

Team Writes Recommendations For Regular Programs

For those students who are not eligible or in need of special education and/or related services, the Child Study Team may write recommendations for regular education personnel to utilize for educational planning. These recommendations can be written in the form of an IEP: Total Service Plan.

Team Develops IEP: Total Service Plan

For each student eligible and in need of special education and/or related services, the Child Study Team will develop an IEP: Total Service Plan. This overall plan will reflect expectations on a long-term annual basis. The Total Service Plan will specify placement recommendations and will also designate persons who will be responsible for developing and carrying out specific Implementation/Instructional Plans.

The educational placement recommendation on the Total Service Plan should reflect the service areas listed on the Total Service Plan rather than categorical labels or placement options which may reflect administrative convenience. . .

. . .rather than child-centered needs.

Team Obtains Parental Approval For The IEP: Total Service Plan And For Educational Placement

Although parents must be invited to participate as members of the Child Study Team in educational decision-making concerning their child, it is anticipated that some parents may not wish to be involved in the development of the Total Service Plan.

However, before a particular educational placement and Total Service Plan are initiated, the Child Study Team must secure written parental consent.

Team And Other Appropriate Personnel Develop And Carry Out IEP: Implementation/Instructional Plans

The Child Study Team will retain ultimate responsibility for developing and carrying out IEP: Implementation/ Instructional Plans. Whenever the Child Study Team feels the Implementation Plan is not reflecting the needs of the student (long-term goals, short-term objectives, etc.) . . .

. . .both the Implementation Plan and the Total Service Plan should be reviewed and revised as needed.

As stated previously, an Implementation/Instructional Plan will include short-term objectives which will help the child accomplish long-term, annual goals. Weekly, monthly, or bi-annual short-term objectives may be selected.

In addition, major strategies, specific teaching techniques, materials and resources, and a date for initiation and completion of objectives must be specified for each long-term goal and short-term objective. Criteria will also be provided for the evaluation of short-term objectives and annual goals.

Team May Conduct Or Support Ongoing Monitoring Of The IEP: Total Service Plan And Implementation/Instructional Plans

The appropriateness of the Total Service Plan is reflected in the quality of the Implementation Plans. Ongoing student monitoring will determine the appropriateness of long-term goals, short-term objectives, specific teaching materials, teaching strategies, etc.

Team Conducts Annual Review For Each Student

On an annual basis, the appropriateness of a child's educational program as outlined in the Total Service Plan and the Implementation Plan must be determined. Should parents choose not to participate in the Annual Review of the educational progress of their child, they must be notified of the review outcome. If the Annual Review indicates a full-time regular education placement is appropriate, additional evaluation is needed, and/or a change of special education or related services is warranted, parents must provide written consent.

Team Evaluates Its Effectiveness

One of the major activities of any Child Study Team is to evaluate overall team functioning. Organizational and operational procedures may change as a result of this ongoing evaluation.

The purpose of this book has been to facilitate an understanding of the concept of Individualized Educational Programs and the process for their implementation. It is my hope that it has provided you with insight regarding the functions of a Child Study Team and the process this team must use in order to develop adequate IEP's for our exceptional children.

REFERENCES

Functions of the placement committee in special education. Washington, D.C.: National Association of State Directors of Special Education, 1976.

Russell, F., Shoemaker, S., McGuigan, C., & Bevis, D. *IEP: Individual education programming.* Boise: Idaho State Department of Education, November 1976.

Zeller, R.W. *Perspectives on the individualized education program of P.L. 94-142.* (Working Paper No. 24, Northwest Special Education Learning Resources System). Eugene, Oregon: University of Oregon, December 1976.

About the Editor

Thomas N. Fairchild has his Ph.D. in School Psychology and is currently an Assistant Professor of Guidance and Counseling and Coordinator of the School Psychology Training Program at the University of Idaho. Dr. Fairchild earned his Bachelors, Masters, and Specialist degrees at the University of Idaho. He received his Ph.D. from the University of Iowa in 1974. The editor has published over a dozen journal articles in the areas of school psychology and counseling. Dr. Fairchild has worked as a teacher, counselor, and school psychologist. He has had the privilege of working with students across all grade levels, and in his opinion they are all special.

About the Author

Judy A. Schrag, Ed.D., is a special educator and State Director of Special Education in Idaho. She earned her Bachelor's Degree from the University of Kansas, her Master's Degree from the University of Idaho, and her Ed.D. at the University of Idaho in 1972. Her professional experience includes regular and special education, classroom teaching, program development, and program administration. Dr. Schrag has served as consultant and evaluator for federal projects serving handicapped children. She has also served as a consultant for several states in developing special education policies and practices. She has been a resource person for several Bureau of Education for the Handicapped and Council for Exceptional Children projects and activities, and is currently serving as a member of the Executive Board of the National Association of State Directors of Special Education (NASDSE). She has authored several articles, documents, and grants in the area of special education. Judy and her family also spend many hours hiking, fishing, and in general enjoying the Sawtooth Mountains of Idaho.

About the Illustrator

Anyone can draw, but to be a good illustrator one must have three things: First, one needs a keen awareness of life in order to keep a running file of personal experiences for future reference; second, one needs a personal style or technique of drawing established and refined by time. For example, the technique of *line economy* is important. This is the knack of creating expressions or poses with a minimum use of line. And third, but most importantly, an illustrator must have *fun* while drawing, for if he does, it will show in his work so that others will enjoy it too.

The illustrator of this book possesses all of these qualities and more. He is Bart Miller, a fourth year Architecture major at the University of Idaho. He works on campus as a graphic artist. "I love to draw; especially kids and animals," he says. His major goal is to become an architect, but he also hopes to illustrate a series of children's books. Until then he hopes you enjoy this book.